8 Minute Maverick

Section 8 Real Estate Strategies for Financial Triumph

Andre Calloway-Cazares

IME Publishing Group
1990 N California Blvd. Suite 20 PMB 1065
Walnut Creek, California 94596

1-866-726-6563

www.IMEPublishingGroup.com

Andre Calloway-Cazares -1st ed.

Section 8 Free Housing Calculator

Use my *Section 8 Rental Property Calculator* to identify how many rental properties you require to pay for your monthly housing expense. This allows you to live for free.

https://bit.ly/3YdzTtI

Chapter 1

Introduction

WELCOME TO *8 MINUTE MAVERICK*. First, I want to thank everyone for purchasing the book. You've decided to create passive income and a real estate business on the side that will be cash flow positive and eventually be able to take care of your housing and possibly retire you. This book aims to help you with a step-by-step process of analyzing cash flow positive Section 8 properties to help you achieve financial freedom.

Everyone's definition of financial freedom is different. Some people want to send their kids to private schools, and some want to pay for their housing, rent, or mortgage. Some people want Lambos and jets. All those things are achievable. You get to decide what financial freedom looks like for you.

I enjoy the fact that my rental properties take care of my housing. I live in Los Angeles in a luxury apartment by the beach. This was possible through real estate and technology. It was impossible to purchase properties remotely 10 or 15 years ago. However, in my book and course, Section 8 in 8 Minutes, I will show you how to do this step-by-step with all the necessary tools.

First, let's talk about who I am. My name is Andre Calloway-Cazares, and I've been doing real estate as a side hustle since 2016. I started with Airbnb in New York City when I moved there. Eventually, I purchased four Airbnbs that I managed remotely, two in Iowa and two in Atlanta, Georgia. I learned a ton from that process and switched real-estate strategies. I now own $3 million worth of cash-flowing rental properties out of state using my Section 8 model and strategies.

Growing up, my family on both sides utilized many government assistant programs, such as Section 8, Welfare, WIC, and Food Stamps. When people think about Section 8, they think, "Oh gosh, these are the worst people." I don't have that perspective because I grew up using these programs. I vividly remember standing in the WIC line to get cereal and milk with my mom.

I started my work career 15 years ago by selling cell phones at the T-Mobile kiosk in Ontario Mills Mall in California. Then, after an exhausting nine years of working in retail, not having weekends off, working every holiday, and being underpaid, I finally got my big break and moved up into corporate sales in New York City. But I quickly learned that making $100,000 still wasn't enough to live comfortably, as I was still living paycheck to paycheck.

I researched Airbnb, four-unit FHA multifamily, and senior assisted living homes. I started with multiple Airbnbs, but I eventually settled on Section 8 properties for many reasons. All of this was in pursuit of passive income and peace of mind because I couldn't keep working how hard I was while barely living paycheck to paycheck.

In the coming chapters, you'll learn, step by step, the process I used to remotely analyze Section 8 real estate properties, which will help you achieve your financial goals. First, let's understand Section 8.

Section 8 is a federal housing assistance program in the United States. It is managed by the U.S. Department of Housing and Urban Development (HUD). The program provides housing vouchers to low-income families, elderly individuals, and people with disabilities so they can afford decent and safe housing.

The U.S. government often pays up to 100% of your tenant's rent each month, typically around 80% to 90%, but some tenants qualify for 100% payments. In many markets, the government will pay you around 20% to 30% more monthly rent than the current market rent, which impacts your return on investment. For example, in specific markets where I invest, like St. Louis, if a house gets $1,000 a month for the market rent, I typically will get $1,300 a month for selecting a tenant on Section 8, which increases your return.

The government incentivizes landlords and investors to offer safe and affordable housing for guaranteed rents and higher rental amounts. As an investor in lower-income areas, I find it best not to deal with market tenants as they don't always pay on time. Getting guaranteed income directly deposited on the first of the month, and it being a higher amount than a market tenant would be, is a good exchange, and it's why you would want to do Section 8. The other reason I love Section 8 is because of the lower turnover. Your highest rental expense typically will be when tenants move out of your home, as you then have to get the property ready for the next tenant to move in.

A Section 8 tenant stays twice as long on average as a market tenant. If you can get a tenant in and they stay for three to five years, you don't have to incur that cost of turning over that rental property. Additionally, you have more leverage as a landlord when you accept the housing vouchers.

For example, in the markets where I invest, in St. Louis and the Midwest, it takes two to three years to get on the housing voucher program. You can't just say, "Hey, I want a Section 8 voucher." There's a very intense interview and screening process, and it can take several years to get a voucher. Once you get the voucher, you have a six-month timeframe to use it. Otherwise, if you don't use it on a property, you lose your voucher. You then must reapply and go through the entire process again.

I've rented to multiple tenants, and it typically wasn't their first time going through the process. Often, they've gone through the two-year process and tried to get a property within six months, but failed. It's very common to reapply for the voucher program due to not finding a property within the six-month timeframe.

If you're getting on the Section 8 program in California, the waiting list is eight years. Tenants are more likely to treat your house nicely and are great to work with because this voucher program is critical to their livelihood.

Higher rents on your properties *can* mean a higher appreciation for your portfolio valuation. I have 21 properties now. Since each unit generates income, I could get a much higher valuation if I ever wanted to sell my entire portfolio. I can sell it based on the generated income. Typically, single-family homes will appreciate or appraise based on the comps and the surrounding houses. That's usually the case for single-family homes. But if you have 8, 12, 15, or 20 houses, they've now looked at your portfolio as an asset. Therefore, it matters how much rent your property generates. That's how you can get a higher valuation on your portfolio, but this is not usual in single-family homes.

Section 8 Myths

Section 8 tenants will destroy your property. Any tenant can destroy your property—regular market tenants, Section 8, friends, family—it just doesn't matter. Which is why I will show you an in-depth tenant screening process to avoid these mistakes. I've had a couple of evictions because I missed things. I'll show you exactly what I missed, so you don't make that mistake.

The idea that Section 8 tenants are terrible people is untrue. Remember, my family on both sides used Section 8, so I know how friendly and good these people can be.

Section 8 tenants won't pay their rent. The U.S. government pays 80 to 90% of the rent, sometimes 100%. We have a more significant issue if the U.S. government can't pay the rent. The other thing that is most important about the government paying the rent is you are not on the same terms for filing evictions as if it were a market tenant. If a tenant is not paying their portion, you are given their caseworker's contact information and you can contact the caseworker, and if they are causing a nuisance or issues to your property. The caseworker can remove them from the government assistance program. If they get removed from the program, it is for life. Tenants know this and they are delighted to only pay a portion of the rent, which may be $75 out of $1,000 rent, or they may only be responsible for $50 or $75. The tenants don't want to lose that perk, which is why I find they are much more cooperative than a market tenant.

Section 8 tenants can't be trusted. This is false. Section 8 tenants are ordinary people like you and me who are elderly or disadvantaged due to having a disability, and they can't work or do not make enough income, things like that. Many people look at Section 8 tenants as bad, disgusting people, and that's just not the case at all. I love working with my Section 8 tenants. They remind me of my family, and I can relate to the struggle. Also, not sure if this means anything to anyone, but I enjoy taking money from the government. Let's be honest, capitalism hasn't always been ethical, and I sleep better at night knowing the government is now paying me. *Oh, how the tables have turned.* That is a perk that I can't quantify.

In the old way, you used to purchase real estate only where you lived. However, since 50% of Americans are considered to be in high-cost- of-living areas, it may not be possible to purchase a property within that state. If you're looking to retire and produce cash-flowing properties quickly, you're likely going to need to open up your mentality and invest out of state. I live in California and the rent to price ratio makes little sense. I'll explain further in my real estate course why it doesn't make sense and provide the returns. The numbers will make this very clear.

Most first-time investors do not have hundreds of thousands of dollars to invest. That's what it's going to cost to get started in a place like California. But when you're investing out of state, you can buy a conventional property for as low as $15,000 out of pocket.

This is significantly less than the $100,000—$200,000 you would need in California or a place like New York. Also, there's just going to be more inventory available. Less competition out of state just means more homes available, and then you can widen your search to multiple markets.

I started in St. Louis, but I also worked in Iowa and Atlanta. Other popular markets include Memphis, Kansas City, Detroit, and Birmingham, Alabama. There are so many places where you can invest and scale quickly.

Another significant reason for out-of-state investing is the tenant-landlord laws. In Los Angeles, where I live, we have rent control laws, meaning you can't raise the rent to the desired amount. Also, in some situations, if a tenant plays it right, they can stay in your home for up to a year without paying rent.

California has too many tenant-friendly laws, which is why I prefer to invest in the Midwest. I prefer to stick to states like Missouri, Alabama, and Texas. They're very landlord-friendly and allow quick evictions. For example, in Missouri, it takes four to six weeks to evict someone, which is unheard of in places like California. Additionally, Missouri has very low property taxes.

Chapter 2

Investing 101

BEFORE I SHOW YOU HOW TO ANALYZE THESE PROPERTIES, I want to set some guidelines. Many of you reading this book don't know what you're targeting or looking for when investing. Let's set a baseline for what is a good investment. Generally, 10% is considered a good return on investment. That means if I invest $10,000 on January 1st, a 10% return means I now have $11,000 by December 31st. It does not mean that I made $11,000, but that I made $1,000 on my $10,000 investment.

So, 10% of $10,000 is $1,000, meaning I still have my $10,000 plus an extra $1,000, giving me $11,000 by December 31st of that year. For example, had you invested $10,000 in Apple stock from April 2023 through April 2024, with a 6% return, you would end up with $10,600 in total. You have your initial $10,000, plus the 6% return, which is $600. Your total investment is now worth $10,600.

In the same timeframe, the S&P 500 is up to 24%. That's a phenomenal year. You put in $10,000 in April 2023, and it's up 24%. That means now you've earned $2,400 on your $10,000, which is a total worth of $12,400. I hope everyone can understand this. I want to set that baseline to know what we're targeting.

On Section 8 rental properties, I target a minimum 20% return. I target higher returns because of the higher risk I'm taking. When I invest in Apple or the S&P 500, it's as simple as pressing a button on Robinhood to buy shares. Apple handles everything-managing real estate, employees, and production. I don't have to lift a finger, yet I own a piece of the company. This investment is incredibly passive; I put in zero effort but benefit from a return of around 6% just by choosing the right company.

Section 8 and real estate require less effort than holding a traditional job, but they still demand more work than simply investing in Apple stock or the S&P 500. As a result, I expect a higher return to justify the additional risk and effort involved.

A lot of other real estate gurus and people will sell you on a 5% or 7% return. Or they'll tell you, *oh, you're going to get a 30% return*, but they're likely calculating other things like expected appreciation or expected equity over the next year, debt pay down, and so on and so forth.

Here's an example: if I put in $10,000 for a property, I need to profit at least $2,000 when I underwrite my deals to make sure I get a 20% return. I just wanted to set the level before we get started.

Chapter 3

Finding Section 8 Properties

Before we dive into properties, let's first explore how to identify a promising market. Then, based on the criteria I provide, you'll be equipped to determine which market aligns best with your investment goals.

The first thing to look for is population size. I target population sizes over 200,000. For example, in St. Louis, where I invest, it has a population size of 300,000. The surrounding metropolitan area is about 3 million, which is a very healthy population size. In the past, I made the mistake of investing in an area with a low population size. I had two Airbnbs in Dubuque, Iowa, which has a city population of 15,000. Even though the Airbnbs were profitable, I had a lot of issues with staffing, getting cleaners, and handling maintenance requests. I let go of those properties because I couldn't find adequate staffing. I now stay away from small populations because if you're doing this remotely, you have to be able to call and have a situation fixed immediately. Typically, you can find whatever you need in a place with a population of 3 million people.

If you're in person, and you want to be highly hands-on and do it yourself, you don't have to avoid small populations, you might find that, since you're doing all the work, it's not a big deal to take care of things yourself. Economic data shows you need to have your house in an area with plenty of jobs. You want your tenants to find another job if they lose the one they have. You want the average person to find a job that pays them enough to afford a home.

Next, you'll look at crime. Now, crime occurs everywhere, but you need to find out how much you're comfortable with. This can be very difficult to gauge. However, I have an excellent system that's helped me combat crime issues. We're dealing with Section 8 properties, and typically properties under $100,000, which can mean higher crime. You just have to find out what works for you.

I start by going to bestplaces.net. I have a premium plan on this website, which costs $10 a month, but there are other crime sites available. We're going to look at St. Louis, Missouri. The first thing I will look at is population size. You want to target metropolitan areas.

The population is 2.8 million, that's a significant population size. Next, you want to make sure there's job growth (+19% for St. Louis). The unemployment rate is 4.8%. It's below the U.S. average, which is excellent. Jobs have also increased by 1%. Next, you'll look for population growth. The population in St. Louis was 2.5 million 30 years ago, which means it's grown by 300,000.

Overall, St. Louis has job growth, low unemployment, and affordable housing. St. Louis is known for its affordability, making it a promising area for economic growth. Investing in property here can lead to rising property values and rents. As inflation increases and more people move into the area, the demand for housing rises. With a growing population comes the need for more homes, as families are formed, and housing becomes a limited resource. This dynamic drives up housing costs and property values. However, not every neighborhood follows this trend, which is why we'll explore additional metrics later in the book to help you make more informed decisions.

We now have the population size and economic data. Now, let's look at the crime. I'm going to compare St. Louis County versus St. Louis Metro. In St. Louis, the city, violent crime is four times the U.S. average of 22, which is exceptionally high. It doesn't get much worse than that. Maybe Detroit and Memphis are worse.

Property crime and violent crime are both essential to help us invest remotely because your property may remain vacant for a period of time.

Per my experience, you don't want to be in an area with a lot of crime because it means higher theft and they can steal some costly items like water heaters and air conditioning units.

Now, let's compare crime in St. Louis Metro. In St. Louis Metro, the crime rate is about the same as the national average. However, the property crime rate for St. Louis Metro is less than half that of St. Louis City. A useful tip is to analyze the crime rate in an area that you are familiar with to help give you context. For example, I live in Santa Monica, California. The crime rate here is 21. This helps me to better understand the crime rate metrics and score.

How to Pick a Market

I use an interactive map that I show in my course, *Section 8 in 8 Minutes*, which displays violent and property crime in St. Louis County. In the St. Louis downtown area, the violent crime is 86 and property crime is 85 (out of 100). I'm going to compare the crime rate in the surrounding areas. Let's start with Jennings, where I bought my first property. Jennings has a crime score of 70 and 71. Next to Jennings we have Bellefonte and Spanish Lake, which have a crime score of 35 and 27. What does this tell you about crime? It tells you that there's a concentrated amount of crime deeper in the heart of the city. You determine what you're comfortable with.

Another useful website is spotcrime.com. This website shows you recent crimes that have happened in your neighborhood. You can look up recent crimes like shootings and robberies, and this may help steer you away from potential bad investment properties.

This is how to analyze crime remotely at a high-level overview. It has worked well for me.

Chapter 4

The 5-Star Property Review

Now, let's discuss the five-star property review. We typically aim for properties rated four stars or higher, and I'll outline the criteria for you. Once you've selected your market and specific area, it's important to examine your chosen property using Google Street View. Make sure to check certain aspects before submitting offers, placing bids, or scheduling inspections.

The following are the five things you should look for on Google Street View. Again, we want properties with four stars and above. If during your Google Street review, you see the following items, you must deduct a star from the total score.

Boarded-up businesses or windows nearby or on the same street as the property. If you see this, you must deduct a star.

Manicured lawns or nice curb appeal. I stay away from places that are not manicured or lawns that are not kept.

Avoid major streets and metropolitan areas. I prefer a cul-de-sac or suburban neighborhood. Why do I want that? Because that's what Section 8 tenants are looking for.

Suburban areas typically have less crime and since I'm an out-of-state investor, I want to remove as much risk as possible. I'm looking for properties that are not in the city.

I also pay attention to the cars in the area, looking for *trap* cars as opposed to family vehicles.

Additionally, I'm cautious about seeing multiple cars parked at a single residence. A high number of vehicles can indicate many people living in close quarters, which may increase the potential for conflicts or other issues due to the density of the population.

I use spotcrime.com and check for shootings and crimes on the same street.

If you pass these items, you have a five-star property. Again, as a remote investor, I'm all about removing risk from afar. That's why I created this five-star property review metric to help you find the best property. My course, Section 8 in 8 Minutes, provides real-life examples with complete walkthroughs.

Chapter 5

What to Look for in a Perfect Section 8 Home

Part 1

WE WILL DETERMINE WHAT TO LOOK FOR IN A PERFECT Section 8 home. If you're a first-time investor, which I assume many of you reading this book are, you will want to start with vacant turnkey properties on MLS, Zillow, Redfin, Trulia, and other similar websites. Many people get caught up in the craze or buzz of off-market deals or seller-financed properties.

You will want to follow the step-by-step guide. When you're starting out, off-market and seller-financed deals add a level of complexity, especially if you are remote. If you are in person, you may take an off-market or creative finance deal because it's easier to manage that risk. When out-of-state investing, you must remove as much risk as possible. The next thing to look for are three- and four-bedroom properties with only one bath, two full baths at a maximum. This is because Section 8 requires just one full bathroom per property. You don't get any extra credit for a second bathroom. I typically look for properties with two full bathrooms because tenants like having separate bathrooms, and typically, the three-bedroom and two-bath or the four-bed, two-bath, or four- bed, 1.5-bath, go right away.

You can have that property rented or receive multiple applications within the first day. You might wonder if the number of bedrooms matters when purchasing an investment property, and the answer is definitely *yes*. Section 8 provides payment based on a scale of one to four bedrooms, with each category having different rental rates. You'll typically see the best returns in the three- and four-bedroom range. While there are a few five-bedroom properties available, they are less common.

I have two tenants using a five-bedroom voucher on my four- bedroom home, and I'm still getting more money on some other properties that only have a four-bedroom voucher. That's something to be aware of. You'll want to start with a one-story home of 800 to 1,400 max square feet.

I recommend starting with a one-story home between 800 and 1,400 square feet. However, if you're just beginning, it's best to keep your target closer to 1,000 square feet. Larger homes can involve more maintenance and a more complex turnover process. I've included the 1,400-square-foot option for those of you with more experience, as we're also considering factors beyond just cash flow.

We're also looking for appreciating properties. Typically, properties that you can refinance and get money back are going to be bigger. However, you can still cash out or refinance smaller properties. When you're getting started, you want to have a one-story home, 800 to 1,000 square feet. You can find smaller three-bedroom homes with 700 to 750 square feet, but I recommend avoiding these properties. They're just too tiny and harder to rent on Section 8.

When starting out, you want to be around 5,000 to 10,000 max lot size. Five thousand square feet for a lot size is typically the smallest lot size in most markets.

The highest you want to go is 10,000 sq. ft. lot size. You also want to stick to a one-story property. The reason is that a two-story, 1,500-square-foot home on a one-acre lot generates the same amount of rent for Section 8. We are looking to get the most bang for our buck. There's no point in getting a more expensive home. Typically, a bigger home costs more money, but for Section 8, it does not mean that you will generate more money.

Next, let's look at the HVAC system, roof, and water heater. You want to make sure these items are under ten years or new is preferred. When you do your property inspection, typically, your licensed inspector is going to check the age of all the electrical panels, the HVAC. It's crucial to check the condition of the HVAC system, water heater, and the roof before purchasing a property. These are significant expenses, and if they need replacement, it can significantly impact your overall investment costs, as you'll need to set aside funds for these updates.

Next, we will review the HUD Fair Market Rent (FMR) https://www.huduser.gov/portal/datasets/fmr/fmrs/FY20 25_code/select_Geography.odn to ensure Section 8 rental rates are at or above 1.5% rent-to-price ratio. For example, if a property costs $100,000, then I'm looking for the HUD FMR Section 8 rental rate to be at $1,500/month or more ($1,500 is 1.5% of $100,000).

When starting out, it's best to avoid off-market deals, especially if you're working remotely. Stick to platforms like Zillow, Redfin, and the MLS—I highly recommend this approach. I built my entire portfolio using MLS. Initially, I attempted a subject to/creative financing strategy after hearing pitches like "You can get a house for only $3,000 down." After six months of trying to purchase a creative-finance property, I realized it was too challenging, especially remotely. That said, I believe this strategy can work well for those operating locally.

Back to looking at the perfect property. I recommend you avoid garages or detached garages when you're starting out. As this costs extra maintenance. Additionally, tenants often accumulate a large amount of belongings, which can significantly increase the cost of cleaning out the property after they move out. The more items that need to be removed, the higher the haul-away expenses. Detached garages and sheds become storage spaces for all sorts of things. You don't want that when starting out. Section 8 does not pay you additionally if you have a garage or not. However, once you gain more experience and are looking for a cash-out refinance, you may decide to take on the risk and purchase a property with a garage.

I'm providing you with the criteria to guide your decisions. While some aspects can be adjusted and not everything may align perfectly, these are the key data points you should keep in mind as you evaluate your options.

Your typical three-tab shingle roof lifespan is around 20 years, depending on the condition. I'd recommend using better material, but it may make more financial sense to go with a cheaper option. Again, you get to decide what works best for you and your budget.

The average lifespan of an HVAC system is also ten years. Which is why it's best to look for a property with a newer system. You can get a detailed HVAC inspection for around $100-$200, but prices will vary based on the area.

I recommend getting an inspection from a licensed inspector. These typically cost around $300, with additional fees for services like sewer inspections, radon tests, and more. When you're just starting out, I advise against purchasing properties with foundation or basement leak issues. The worst property I ever bought had a significant basement problem, and I initially underestimated how serious it would be. I ignored it, and it ended up costing me $22,000 to fix the issue. Had I followed this process in this book, I would have easily backed out of that deal. As the house was only $55,000 but I spent well over $22,000 to fix the issues.

In hindsight, I realize I overlooked the basement issues because I live in California, where basements aren't common, so I didn't fully understand their significance or how expensive they can be to repair. I've since learned that basements are a specific type of foundation, which is more common in the Midwest, where I do most of my investing. As a result, I missed recognizing the problems in the basement. This is an example of how you could have an inherent bias which could impact your investment decision-making. That's why the information in this book is so critical if you are open to investing out-of-state where the standards are likely different from where you live and what you are used to.

Everything's fixed now, and I learned a great deal from that property. Please do not buy any properties with foundation issues, especially when buying them turnkey. This house was supposed to be a turnkey property.

From the outside, the property looked great, but it was like seeing someone with Instagram filters on and then meeting them in person—it was a completely different story. It was only my third property, so I didn't have as much experience, and I ended up wasting $22,000 on something that could have easily been avoided.

You should also get a termite inspection. My licensed inspector includes a termite report as part of the overall inspection, complete with photos. He'll indicate whether termites were present in the past and can even estimate the time frame, like, "Termites haven't caused damage here in a few years," or "There are active termites." Regardless, he always recommends spraying as a precaution.

Spraying your house once a year costs about $80, so it's incredibly affordable. If your inspector doesn't do it, you'll have to call a local pest report company, or your property manager can provide you with a vendor.

Let's talk about siding. Ideally, look for vinyl siding, as it's much easier to maintain and replace. Wood siding can become soft, deteriorate, or wear down over time, leading to more issues.

Plumbing has caused me countless headaches, which is why I now do a camera inspection of every sewer line—I no longer skip this step. Before I started investing, my only experience with plumbing issues was a clogged toilet, so I didn't realize how serious plumbing problems could be and overlooked these inspections early on. During a plumbing check, they typically look for things like rust or corrosion on water heaters, leaky faucets, or sinks, water damage, any type of leaks, and uncovered holes where the pipes enter.

Flooring—I rarely replace flooring unless I absolutely have to. Section 8 does not pay you extra to have nicer or better flooring. Now, sometimes you have to replace a carpet if it's in terrible shape or pet stains as those stains and odors are difficult to remove. I prefer installing luxury vinyl flooring, which, while slightly more expensive than carpet or laminate, offers much greater durability. It's waterproof, looks more upscale, and provides a luxury feel. I've used luxury vinyl in about half of my properties, and now, any home I remodel automatically gets vinyl flooring.

For electrical systems, ensure that every outlet, both inside and outside, is functioning properly and grounded. Have your property manager or inspector use an electrical tester to test each outlet. The Section 8 inspection will check for this as well. They use an electrical tester that lights up red if the outlet is grounded correctly. A properly functioning electrical system is critical, and this includes having an up-to-date electrical panel. Your inspection report should detail the condition of the panel. If it's an older Zinsco or Federal Pacific panel, it needs to be replaced immediately, as these panels are known for failing, which has caused thousands of fires. Replacement costs range between $2,000 and $4,000, depending on the property.

If you have one of those older electrical panels that are known to fail, you cannot get insurance on the house. If you can't get insurance on the house, you can't get a mortgage. You'd have to buy the house in cash. The newer electrical panels will help you pass inspections, allow you to obtain home insurance and overall, it's safer for tenants and helps you preserve your investment.

For windows, it's essential to ensure that each one functions correctly. Verify that they open, close, and lock without any issues. It's important to have every window checked, as Section 8 will inspect them as well. Make sure that each window has a screen; this is crucial for safety in case of a fire. In an emergency, windows must operate smoothly to allow a quick escape.

****EXPERT BONUS TIPS****

Here are some expert tips for inspecting a home. If you purchased a property before placing a tenant, consider removing the dishwasher. Dishwashers can be costly to maintain, and if one is present when a tenant moves in, you are responsible for its upkeep. Since dishwashers often break down and usage can vary widely, I always opt to remove them and replace them with a cabinet instead. It's a much more affordable option.

You are also responsible for providing the oven and refrigerator. I typically install a basic refrigerator—the most affordable model I could find at Home Depot. It simply opens and closes, featuring a bottom fridge compartment and a top freezer section.

I avoid refrigerators with built-in ice and water dispensers because of the extra maintenance they require. Section 8 won't cover these costs, and if the tenant moves in with one already installed, you'll be responsible for any issues that arise.

You can also remove ceiling fans and install mount flush lights. Only a couple of my properties have ceiling fans, and I forgot to remove them when I purchased the properties. I haven't had any issues with them, but they may arise in the future.

The goal is to keep your properties as simple and low-maintenance as possible, while still providing quality housing. For example, we prioritize homes without garages and prefer slab foundations over basements, as basement water leaks can be costly to repair. We also remove dishwashers, garbage disposals, and ceiling fans, and opt for refrigerators without built-in water or ice dispensers to minimize potential upkeep expenses.

Congratulations! By ensuring your property is equipped with the right features, you've successfully eliminated a significant portion of potential maintenance requests that could have eaten into your profits.

Chapter 6

Financing Section 8 Properties

IN THIS CHAPTER, WE WILL COVER ONE OF THE BIGGEST questions regarding Section 8 properties: how to finance properties.

Your first option should be conventional loans, as they offer the easiest financing for investment properties. These loans, backed by Fannie Mae and Freddie Mac, typically come with the lowest fees and interest rates. Plus, they allow you to take out up to 10 mortgages. I've already maxed out the 10-mortgage limit, so I now use adjustable-rate mortgages, but you'll want to start with conventional loans, which require full documentation.

That means they will ask you for your paycheck stubs, proof of employment, tax returns, LLC tax returns, bank accounts, and business bank accounts. They're going to ask for everything, including your LLC operating agreement. That's what a full-doc loan means. With this option, you can buy a duplex, triplex, or fourplex with one loan.

One strategy could be to use each loan to purchase fourplexes, giving you 40 units across ten mortgages. However, I don't recommend using Section 8 for fourplexes. I prefer not to have Section 8 tenants living in close proximity, as many are either not working or are disabled and spend much of their time at home. I find it better to have more space between tenants in those situations.

Another option, especially for those without a steady income or the required documentation, is a DSCR loan (Debt Service Coverage Ratio Loan). With this type of loan, the lender focuses on the property's rental income compared to the mortgage payment. For example, if your mortgage is $700 and the rent (such as Section 8 rent) is $1,400, that gives you a 2.0 DSCR. Lenders typically look for a ratio of at least 1.25, meaning if your monthly mortgage is $700, they would want the rent to be at least $950.

The downside of this type of loan is that it comes with more risk, making it less straightforward than a conventional loan, and you'll end up paying higher fees. You may also encounter challenges with lenders who won't approve loans for properties under $100,000. Securing financing for properties below this threshold can be difficult, though some lenders offer it—but be prepared for higher costs when doing so.

Another issue with DSCR loans is that when you acquire a property, you don't get to set the rent amount—it's determined by an appraiser. For example, even if Section 8 pays $1,400 a month, the appraiser might estimate the rent at $850 or $900, and that's the number the lender will use. However, if you're doing a DSCR cash-out refinance with an existing Section 8 tenant paying $1,400, the lender will accept that amount after verifying it through your bank statements. I don't prefer DSCR loans for acquisitions because the rent is up to the appraiser, but if it's your best option, it's worth considering.

Then there are commercial loans, which are typically used for properties with five or more units, like apartment investing. However, some commercial lenders will also finance single- family homes. However, some commercial lenders only offer 20-year amortization, which leads to higher monthly payments.

Another option is portfolio loans, which are often considered a type of commercial loan and have gained popularity in the past few years. These loans typically aren't offered by large banks like Bank of America, Chase, or Wells Fargo. Instead, I recommend looking into small, local community banks. When contacting them, ask if they are investor-friendly and if they offer loans under $100,000—those are my key questions. It's also worth reaching out to local credit unions to see if they provide residential loans under $100,000. If they don't, ask for referrals; that's how I found my lender. A credit union referred me to a bank that fit my needs.

These types of loans are usually fixed for 30 years, but with an adjustable-rate mortgage, the interest rate changes after a set period—typically five, seven, or ten years. Initially, I was hesitant about adjustable-rate mortgages and stuck with conventional loans. However, after reaching the ten-property mortgage limit, I had to explore other options.

I initially feared adjustable-rate mortgages (ARMs) because of the 2008 housing crisis. During the 2008 housing crisis, many borrowers who had taken out ARMs faced significant financial strain because of interest rates resetting to much higher levels after an initial fixed period. This led to widespread foreclosures and a loss of equity for many homeowners. Many homeowners took on ARMs and found themselves unable to refinance as interest rates rose, leading to skyrocketing monthly payments that they could no longer afford. This experience left a negative impression on me. However, I've since reevaluated their benefits, and I'll explain why I now use them.

When you're working with lenders and banks, they really like people who have their business in order, as it's easier and quicker for lenders to process together. You want to have your LLC documents, tax returns, paycheck stubs, W-2s, and the profit-and-loss statement of your properties.

I recommend creating a dedicated folder on your laptop to organize all the necessary documents for applying for a loan. This should include personal financial statements, stock statements, 401(k) statements, paycheck stubs, W-2s, tax returns, and, if applicable, the tax returns for your LLCs. Having these documents readily available allows you to respond quickly when someone requests them, presenting you as organized and prepared. Lenders prefer working with individuals who can provide their documentation promptly; delays can lead to lost opportunities. In my course, Section 8 in 8 Minutes, I offer a comprehensive and detailed explanation of the loan process, complete with real-life examples to enhance your understanding.

What does *investor-friendly* mean? It's essential to ensure your lender permits you to close in with an LLC or transfer the property to an LLC without incurring additional fees. I strongly recommend that you do not hold any rental properties in your personal name; instead, create an LLC to hold your properties. This helps limit your personal liability.

While this may sound straightforward, many lenders impose restrictions, including a *call on loan* clause. This means that if you transfer ownership from your name to an LLC, the lender could demand immediate repayment of the entire loan amount. However, an investor-friendly lender may not enforce this clause. Be sure to discuss the terms of your agreement thoroughly with your lender. Keep in mind financing deals under one hundred thousand dollars is more complicated, but not impossible.

Now, I'm going to show you what an adjustable-rate mortgage is and how it works.

Once I accumulated too many properties, I could no longer secure additional conventional loans after reaching the limit of ten mortgages in my name. As a result, I had to turn to an adjustable-rate mortgage with a 10-6 structure. This means the interest rate is fixed for the first ten years and then adjusts every six months thereafter, starting in year eleven.

Typically, adjustable-rate mortgages have a cap on how high the interest rate can go. For example, my most recent adjustable-rate mortgage has a locked-in interest rate of 6.5% for ten years, with a maximum rate of 11.5% thereafter. In a worst-case scenario, if there was a significant financial downturn, my mortgage payment would rise from $689 to a maximum of $925.

I justified this decision because I currently receive $1,515 in rent for this property. Even in the worst-case scenario, I would still maintain positive cash flow. I have already raised the rent twice on this property, and I expect an average annual rent increase of around $108 each year.

On the flip side, if the government lowers interest rates below 6.5%, such as dropping to 2% like we saw during the COVID-19 pandemic, my payment could decrease to as low as $551. While it's highly unlikely we'll see those historically low rates again, it's important to keep in mind that anything is possible.

When considering riskier loans, it's essential to crunch the numbers. After evaluating the situation, I concluded that this was a risk I was willing to take. I plan to refinance this property before the ten-year mark, but even if I don't, I'll still be in an excellent position, especially since I anticipate raising the rent consistently during that time.

If You Can Afford a Car Payment, You Can Afford an Investment Payment

I have this slogan where I like to say, *if you can afford a car payment, then you can also afford an investment property payment.*

I often receive questions like, "Can I buy a house? Can I invest in property?" Many people feel intimidated by the idea of purchasing a $60,000 or $70,000 home, but financing for a property is often just as accessible as financing for a car. If you're approved for a car loan, you may also qualify for a home loan.

However, if you have significant bankruptcies or a credit score around 500, securing an investment property will be quite challenging. On the other hand, if you have a credit score in the 680 to 690 range and earn $50,000 to $60,000 a year, you may very well be able to obtain an investment property. I'm not suggesting you should rush into it, but I want to make you aware of the criteria lenders typically consider.

How to Get Money for Section 8 Payments

These are the top five ways that I recommend getting money to invest in Section 8.

The first priority should be your savings. I always advise individuals to ensure they are out of survival mode before embarking on real estate investing. If you're still preoccupied with necessities—such as affording gas for your car, putting food on the table, or avoiding disconnection of your cell phone—I believe it's not the right time for you to invest in real estate.

I've shared some of my personal journey with you, and I know firsthand what it means to be in survival mode. I come from a background where we often faced disconnections of our electricity, gas, and internet. This experience drives me to work tirelessly to ensure I never return to that situation. Even as my income has increased, I remain frugal and conservative with my spending. If you're still in survival mode, it's likely that you'll make impulsive decisions when investing in real estate.

Investing in real estate means building wealth slowly. There's no get-rich-quick scheme. This will not replace your job income today. But if you do the work, you follow the step-by-step guide, it will take care of you in the near future. You cannot be in survival mode when you invest.

Another way to get money for Section 8 or any investment is to leverage your job income. I work in corporate technology sales. I tripled my income in three years just by changing three jobs. I built my technology resume. I then hired a professional executive interview coach who helped me negotiate higher salaries during my interviews.

As a result, I increased my earnings from $150,000 in 2019 to $565,000 in 2023, which allowed me to invest significantly more in real estate. Having a strong W-2 income makes it easier for me to secure loans, especially since I already own multiple rental properties.

Many people find security in their jobs and may love what they do, which is fantastic. However, if you aspire to enter the real estate market and replace your job income, I recommend leveraging your current salary by seeking higher-paying opportunities. The best time to look for a new job and negotiate for a raise is when you don't need one. I always kept interviewing, even while I was gainfully employed.

Another option is to borrow from your 401(k). If you're 30 or older, like I am, you may have spent over a decade in your career and accumulated a substantial balance in your 401(k). It's possible to borrow against this amount, but it's essential to conduct a thorough analysis to determine if this approach is viable for you. I recommend considering this option only if you're out of survival mode and are genuinely interested in learning the process and exploring real estate investing.

Your first property isn't going to retire you; it's your tenth property that will. For instance, if you take money from your 401(k) and have a repayment of $500 a month, but your real estate investment generates $500 a month in income, it might seem like a break-even situation. However, the real value lies in the experience and skills you gain through this process, which are far more valuable than just the monthly return. This might mean you have a 401(k) that you can borrow from to help fund your investment journey.

Another option for funding your investments is to tap into your inheritance or support from family members. Many of us have inherited houses or investments, or we may have relatives willing to lend us money. For example, a mentor I admire, whose course I took, began his journey with a $40,000 loan from his parents. He used that money to learn how to fix and flip properties remotely, starting with his first home in Memphis. After completing the renovations, he could do a cash-out refinance. Today, he has successfully flipped over 1,000 properties, and his entire family is now involved in the business. Consider exploring whether family or friends can provide similar support for your investment endeavors.

Other Forms of Financing

I'm sure many of you are familiar with the term *creative financing.* While I want to provide you with unbiased information, it's important to note that, while this is an alternative, it can be challenging. Let me explain.

Before I began purchasing properties, I explored creative and seller financing options. However, I quickly discovered that these deals often involved problematic properties.

To clarify, *seller financing* or *creative financing* refers to situations where the seller or property owner finances the purchase directly without requiring a credit check or going through the traditional mortgage process. Essentially, the seller acts as the bank. For instance, if the seller owns the property outright, they might say, "I'm going to sell you this house for $75,000 with a 10% interest rate."

They get to set the terms, and it's up to you to accept it or not and many people say, "Oh I can get a house for only $2,000 down or $800 down or $1,800 down instead of putting the full 20% down." Although these deals sound too good to pass on, I highly advise you to stay away from these deals.

I learned the hard way after paying a real estate guru $4,000 to help me find a great creative seller-financed property. What I quickly realized was that most seller-financed homes are ones that wouldn't sell through traditional channels like the MLS or Zillow, often because they were in less desirable areas or in poor condition. These properties were essentially the ones that couldn't sell otherwise.

The five-star property review strategy focuses on targeting properties in better, more desirable parts of town. If you're a first-time or remote investor like me, I strongly advise against pursuing creative or seller financed deals. These properties often are in less desirable areas and come with numerous hidden problems. Since the seller sets the terms, they often waive inspections or offer no inspection contingencies, which can be risky. My advice: be cautious of these deals, no matter how attractively they're marketed, as they usually come with a catch.

Based on my experience, I also recommend staying away from subject-to-deals. I paid $7,600 for a subject-to course, aiming to acquire an apartment complex using this strategy. Let me break it down: imagine someone owns an apartment complex with a 30-year fixed mortgage and they've paid off five years, locking in a low 2% interest rate. If they were to sell it now, with the current rates at 7%, the deal wouldn't have cash flow and wouldn't make financial sense.

In a subject-to-deal, the seller can transfer the property to you, and you assume their existing mortgage at the lower interest rate. But here's the catch: you must be re-approved by the lender, and not all loans are assumable—especially with apartments. That's the problem I faced. I came across many sellers, as apartment complexes are struggling with higher interest rates. Apartment financing is usually riskier; most don't have 30-year fixed loans. Instead, they often have floating-rate mortgages or variable terms, like three- or five-year terms. When interest rates spiked recently, those who used commercial financing were hit hard, making these deals even more complicated and risky.

In the residential sector, we don't encounter this as much because we're typically using fixed-rate financing. However, in the commercial space, I saw many deals where lenders required $500,000 down, and I still had to assume the risky floating-rate mortgage. It just didn't make sense for me. If you're a remote or first-time investor, subject-to-deals add an extra layer of complexity that you should avoid. The key is to minimize risk as much as possible, especially when you're starting out.

Private Money

I then paid for a membership for private money. What is private money? Private money is like, "Hey my mom and dad loaned me some money, and I have to pay them back." Then they want 5% extra. Or there are these networks of real estate investors that just have some cash, and they want to make some money on their cash. They'll lend it to you on their own terms. I did also pay for a membership on this, and I tried to get private money for about two to three months and here is my experience trying to secure private money.

I couldn't understand why I couldn't get private money. I had about 14 properties. I had the profit-and-loss statement. Surprisingly, many private money lenders weren't interested in working with me because my credit and financial standing were too strong. They preferred borrowers with worse credit so they could charge higher interest rates and more points. Since I came in prepared and knowledgeable, I heard things like, 'It sounds like you don't even need this money.' It felt a bit sketchy, and after two months of trying, I decided it wasn't the right fit for me. I couldn't understand why, despite my solid credit, financial stability, and experience, they didn't want to move forward. So, I abandoned the private money route.

Chapter 7

Submitting an Offer on a Home

NOW THAT YOU'VE PICKED A MARKET, picked a property, looked at crime, checked whether a property is going to cash flow, and done a ton of your due diligence, we will submit an offer. I want to show you what your offer should include and how to proceed.

When you submit an offer, you want to ask for all the utilities to be connected. Typically, a turnkey property will already have the utilities connected. However, with some discounted properties that have been vacant for a while, the seller may offer them *as-is*, meaning utilities might not be set up, and it's up to you to handle that aspect.

It's crucial to ensure utilities are connected when starting out, especially during colder months. For instance, I once purchased six properties to rehab in the winter, unaware that the pipes had frozen because of a lack of running water. This oversight cost me an additional $1,500 to $5,000 per property in plumbing repairs—expenses that could have been avoided if the utilities had been on and the systems tested beforehand.

Be sure to tell the seller, "I need the utilities to be connected." Have your realtor include this in the contract as part of your 10-day or two-week inspection period. Before submitting your offer, ask your realtor for a quick iPhone walkthrough video to see the property's current condition. This ensures you're not relying solely on the marketing photos, which may not reflect the property as it is today.

It's like seeing someone through Instagram filters versus in real life. Always make sure your realtor sends you a walkthrough video of the property. I've had several instances where I thought I found the perfect property, only to get the video and realize, *No way*. They really dressed it up in the listing photos. Your realtor should typically provide this service for free, though some may charge extra, so be sure to ask upfront.

When submitting your offer, you can select an inspection period that fits your needs—whether it's 48 hours, 5 days, 10 days, two weeks, 10 business days, or 14 days, etc. During this time, you'll arrange for all necessary inspections, such as HVAC, plumbing, and more, to thoroughly assess the property. Choose a timeline that works best for you and allows ample time for these evaluations.

During the inspection period based on the findings, you may decide that this property is not the right fit and decide not to move forward with the purchase. Which is why it's important to always include an inspection period in your offer.

It's essential to include an inspection contingency in your offer. Here are the inspections you should schedule:

1. General Inspection: Conducted by a licensed inspector, this typically costs around $300, though prices may vary by location.

2. HVAC Inspection: This inspection focuses on the heating, ventilation, and air conditioning systems to ensure they are functioning properly.

3. Plumbing Inspections: These typically range from $100 to $200, though prices can vary. This inspection is crucial for properties that have been on the market during the colder months, as vacant homes can have frozen pipes.

4. General Inspection: I usually hire a general contractor to evaluate the property, with costs typically around $100. As you build a relationship with your general contractor and work with them more frequently, they will become familiar with your turnover model. This familiarity allows them to highlight specific issues and provide you with a more tailored inspection that addresses your unique needs.

5. Property Management Inspection: Next, you can have your property manager inspect to assess how turnkey the property truly is. Your property manager will typically charge a trip fee, which you should have negotiated beforehand; expect this to be around $50 to $100. While it's not mandatory, I find that property managers can identify issues that potential future tenants might notice. Since they work closely with tenants, they view the property from a unique perspective that can reveal important insights.

In summary, expect to spend between $600 and $800 for thorough property inspections. While this may seem steep, investing in these inspections can save you significant amounts of money in the long run. For example, if I had conducted these inspections before purchasing the property on Sapphire Avenue, which ultimately cost me $22,000 in repairs, the initial inspection fee would have been a small price to pay. Remember, when buying a property, it's not just about the immediate costs; time is a critical factor as well— delays in fixing issues can lead to escalating expenses. I wish I had prioritized a comprehensive inspection, as it would have helped me avoid costly problems.

Don't cut corners on your first purchase; thorough inspections are a vital part of the learning process. Doing your due diligence will help you avoid unnecessary headaches down the road. I hope these insights assist you as you prepare to submit an offer on a home.

Chapter 8

Property Management

NOW, LET'S DISCUSS PROPERTY MANAGEMENT, which can be quite a challenge. I'm not exaggerating when I say that dealing with property managers will account for about 50% of your effort. Over my five years of acquiring properties and building my real estate portfolio, I've worked with six different property management companies for my Airbnbs and Section 8 properties and have since transitioned to managing my properties myself using various software tools.

I've gained considerable insight into property management practices—what works well and what doesn't. As you scale your portfolio to 20, 30, or even 40+ properties, you may find it necessary to establish your own property management company, as navigating relationships with external managers can be complex. While it's essential to have a property manager when you're starting out—there's really no workaround—I've created a guide and step- by-step blueprint to help you effectively manage your properties.

Even if you're managing properties in person, I strongly recommend hiring a property manager when you first start out. Your initial property is not about blowing it out of the water, it's about gaining valuable insight into the entire process and learning how to navigate it for the first time. Property managers have expertise in various aspects of rental management, including handling evictions, placing tenants, and collecting rent. By working with them, you can absorb as much knowledge and experience as possible, setting a solid foundation for your future investments.

There's a wealth of information about your market that property managers are well-versed in. However, one area where they may lack expertise is in working with Section 8 and navigating the intricacies of the voucher program and its specific requirements. That's where this book comes into play.

Once you finish reading this book, you'll have a deeper understanding of the Section 8 program than most property management companies do. For some reason, many property management firms have not fully tapped into the Section 8 market. Therefore, even if you choose to work with a property management company, you'll still need to be actively involved in managing this aspect. I'll explain what that entails in the following sections.

Let me first explain how a property manager typically operates. They usually charge about 8-10% of the monthly rent—though this is negotiable—for managing the property. This includes handling maintenance and addressing tenant requests. Additionally, they'll charge a one-time fee, usually the equivalent of one month's rent, as a commission for placing a tenant for you.

Now, here's where it gets tricky with Section 8. Property managers often dislike working with Section 8 because it adds extra layers of responsibility, like coordinating additional inspections on top of their usual duties. With so many properties to manage, they don't have the bandwidth to give the level of follow-up needed to navigate the Section 8 bureaucracy. This is why it's crucial for you to stay hands-on and manage the Section 8 tenant placement process yourself. Understanding the pressure property managers face will help you see why your involvement is essential. Property managers often have so many properties that the additional workload from Section 8 can make them hesitant.

Some property management companies may promise to handle the Section 8 process for you, but it typically takes them much longer—often a few months—and they usually charge extra fees for the additional effort. I took on the screening and placement of tenants myself using my system, and I'll walk you through how I do it. Here's why I justified handling it myself:

1) A property manager typically takes 3-4 months to place a Section 8 tenant, and then they charge a full month's rent as a commission. This means I'm looking at about 5 months of zero revenue from the property while still being responsible for the mortgage and other expenses.

2) When I handle tenant screening and inspections myself, it only takes 2-4 weeks. That's why I took the time to learn how to set up all the inspections. Building your own team is essential in the long run to streamline this process and avoid unnecessary delays.

3) Currently (2024), my average rent is $1,503 per month. If I rely on a property manager, it costs me an extra 4 months of lost rent, totaling over $6,000 per property. By handling the process myself, I avoid this significant loss.

4) Let's break it down: $6,000 per property across 21 properties adds up to $126,000 that I would have lost due to using a property management company for tenant screening/placement. That's exactly why I decided to handle it myself.

You can certainly have your property management company handle it, but it's important to set realistic expectations about the process and timelines. Property managers are typically not experts when it comes to Section 8. While some companies may already have Section 8 tenants, many prefer not to deal with the voucher program because it involves a longer, more time-consuming process.

Also, it's crucial to understand that property management companies are essentially sales organizations. Before working with a property management company, I assumed their role was more like that of an assistant, helping me manage properties closely. However, their primary focus is on managing properties at scale, not providing personalized service. You quickly learn that they are motivated by profit, and they take liberty in uplifting costs significantly sometimes.

For example, if you have a $4,000 roof repair, the property management company might add a 20% fee, which means you'd pay an additional $800 for the repair. It's standard practice for property management companies to charge a 10- 20% markup on repairs. However, be cautious—some companies may try to overcharge, inflating costs by 200-300% above standard rates.

When you're just starting out, you likely won't have an established network or contacts, so you may have to pay those extra fees initially—just like I did. However, if you conduct thorough inspections upfront, you can avoid major expenses like replacing a roof, HVAC, or plumbing. I wasn't as diligent with inspections in the beginning, which is why I created this book and the step-by-step guide to help you avoid those costly mistakes.

Here's an example of the financial side of working with a property manager: I had a tree fall and lean against a property, and it took my property manager an entire week to get me a quote—which came back at $2,600. I said, "Absolutely not." I reached out to my contact and got a quote within 24 hours for $950. Every dollar saved is a dollar earned!

This process just doesn't work in the long-term for keeping maintenance costs low or having good tenant satisfaction. I'm paying three times the cost for worse work performed. Property managers typically handle a large volume of properties and often try to tackle multiple requests simultaneously, which can easily cause confusion or mix-ups. This can cause delays and less focus on each property. They also may not provide you with a detailed breakdown of every maintenance request.

They are trying to be in and out as quickly as possible. Now you can understand why working with property management companies is such a headache.

That's why the most successful real estate investors, once they build a sizable portfolio, either hire someone directly to manage their properties or create an in-house team to handle maintenance requests. By the time I got to my fourth property manager, I knew exactly what I needed and negotiated terms accordingly. I told them, "You won't be responsible for placing my tenants. Your role will be to collect rent and handle general management, but I'm not paying 10% of the rent because, with my rent now at $1,500, $1,600, and $1,700, 10% is $150, $160, or $170, it is just too much." Instead, I negotiated the following terms: $100 a month per property. No monthly commission fee because I'm placing the tenant. I pay a $50 trip fee for them to do property showings to potential tenants. I also use their lease, which is an additional $250 fee.

Property managers earn their income through several streams: monthly management fees, marking up the cost of maintenance requests, and commission fees for placing tenants. That's why they're not enthusiastic about handling Section 8 properties, despite the potential for higher rents. The extra inspections and paperwork involved with Section 8 mean double the work for the same pay, which doesn't motivate them.

Another, less obvious, way property managers make money is by holding rent and security deposits in their accounts. Let me explain how this works.

When I first worked with property managers, they were very insistent that my rent and security deposits go into their bank accounts, from which they'd send me my monthly payout. While this is standard practice with property management, I was never fully comfortable with it. I questioned why the rent couldn't be deposited directly into my account instead. Once I understood how the banking system works, I realized that property managers prefer having the rent pass through their accounts because it increases their deposit totals. They can then earn interest on your rent deposits—essentially making free money from your funds.

Property managers can leverage the cash flow from rent deposits to apply for credit lines and other financial tools, as the high volume of money moving through their accounts improves their financial standing. This is entirely legal, and our banking system allows it.

When negotiating with your property manager, it's crucial to understand your business needs so that you can advocate for them. By the time I reached my fourth property manager, I insisted that all rent and security deposits go directly to me; this was nonnegotiable. Initially, this property manager proposed keeping my rent and security deposits, as well as requiring a $1,000 reserve per property.

Consider this: with 21 properties, that would mean $21,000 held in their accounts for property reserves. The security deposits alone would amount to another $21,000, plus over $30,000 in monthly rents being deposited to them. That's a significant sum of money tied up with the property manager that they earn interest on.

Absolutely not! Given my history with terrible property managers and my lack of trust in them, there was no way I could agree to that. I also had no guarantee that I would remain with this property manager long-term given my history and after eight months, I had my recently retired partner manage the properties herself using software and AI tools.

In this chapter, I emphasized the importance of utilizing property managers when starting your investment journey, particularly if you lack a network. I've outlined strategies that have helped me succeed in working with property managers and highlighted potential challenges to be aware of.

You should now have a better understanding of property management companies as I've shared the strategies that I use that allow me to be successful. For further advice, I recommend exploring my course, *Section 8 in 8 Minutes.*

Property Management Interview Guide

Before purchasing a property remotely or in-person you should secure property management first because not all property managers service every area. Before you move forward with a home, use this guide to interview and vet different property managers.

https://bit.ly/3ZX0iNA

Chapter 9

How to Find Section 8 Tenants

NOW THAT WE KNOW HOW TO WORK WITH PROPERTY managers, find a property and other similar topics, we're finding out how to get good, qualified Section 8 tenants. The first thing you'll need to do is find out where the housing authorities are in your market. Type in the housing authority in your market. We already know that in St. Louis, there are two main ones: St. Louis County and then St. Louis Housing Authority. Just call them. You will want to ask if they have an open waitlist. A promising sign of demand is when they have a closed waitlist.

That means there are too many people in the program and not enough houses, so it will be easy to find tenants for your property. Remember, we're targeting five-star properties. These things make your property more valuable and attract more demand. St. Louis has a two- year waiting list, which means it's in extremely high demand. California, like I said earlier, has an eight-year wait list right now. Places like that are in extremely high demand.

Now, the other thing that I would like to ask is whether every market or housing authority uses affordablehousing.com. Mostly everyone's using affordablehousing.com. I can do everything from there. Knowing what I know now, I don't rent my properties outside of affordablehousing.com. A lot of other gurus might say, hey, you can go to Craigslist, you can go to Facebook. But remember, going into Craigslist or Facebook or off-market, we're now adding more risk to the equation.

Remember, you're remote. Or even if you're in person, I want to have it easy-peasy. If you follow the strategy, like having a five-star property, suitable area, lovely home, and so on, you will not have any issue renting your property on affordablehousing.com. When you call the housing authority, you also want to ask them if you need to set up a landlord portal. Sometimes, depending on your housing authority, they might want you in the system first.

In St. Louis, they don't require that. I just send them my landlord information after I select a tenant, and I submit my landlord information on the packet. Once the tenant gets approved, they set up my landlord portal. But some markets might require you to get set up in their system first.

I'm going to explain to you guys how to market your property. Let's go to affordablehousing.com. I'm on the main website as a premium member. This allows me to have a verified badge, which means I submitted documentation to show that I'm a property owner.

A lot of renters send personal information like their taxes, their bank account, and their pay stubs. They want to feel secure. I did not know that this is something that the tenants look at until I spoke with someone. They could see that I was a trusted owner, which gave them more security.

As you post your property, you're the first listing. If somebody else posts their property, then they're the first listing. That's literally how it works. It's sequential. It's not like Instagram or something like that, where the algorithm depends on who you see. No, whoever posts at that time will see the property.

When you're a premium member, you can boost your property to the top of the list, so that's typically what I do. I had a property up for two days, and I had seven people apply and pay the fee without ever seeing the property, which is what you want. You do not want to let people do inspections or viewings before they prove that they're a qualified tenant before they give you the voucher. What I do is when somebody says, "Hey, can I view it first before I pay?" I'm like, "Hi I'm sorry we have a different process, and you must submit a paid application before viewing the property. If you are not ok with this process, we understand and wish you luck on your home search."

I also get professional photos done on every property which comes with a link that lets you do a virtual walkthrough of the home, and I send the link to prospects, which have helped them get a better feel for the home before applying.

You will always want to get professional photos done of your home when you can when it's vacant and let me tell you why.

Once you get a tenant in, you won't be able to get photos of it again in the nicest condition. What if you want to sell it or sell your portfolio? It's going to be very hard to get any wonderful photos that make your property look nice. Now, the tenant's living on this property already, but I have these photos and this link for forever. If I ever wanted to send this to a lender or an investor, or show what my properties look like, I already have this done for all my properties and if a tenant moves out, I already have the professional photos that I can re-upload to rent it out again.

If I ever want to sell my portfolio, it is very easy to just show them what I've got. They understand that this is what it looked like before a tenant moved into it. But at least they could see the quality, see how nice it is, and so on. You need to get professional photos.

I do not market my properties off-site, like Craigslist, Facebook, or anything else, simply because I don't have to. Just like when I earlier covered seller-finance and subject-to, a lot of those properties are outside of what you really want to be doing when you get started. If you're doing this remotely, you want to remove risk as much as possible.

We all know Craigslist and Facebook can be shady. We don't do that. If you can't rent your property after following the five-star review, taking professional photos, and picking a suitable area, then you simply did something wrong. I have had no issues renting. The only problem I've had renting is that a couple of my properties did not fit the five-star review. All my properties that are five-stars, four-stars, have zero issues. But if they're one-star, you'll have problems, like my properties in Jennings. I had issues because they were just in the wrong area and not as desirable.

That's why going through that experience taught me to create this criteria. I started using data, started seeing what tenants wanted and what they were looking for, and realized, *Oh, these are what the tenants are looking for.* That's why I created that five-star property review. Now, if you follow the five-star property review, you've got your professional photos, and you're marketing on affordable housing, you should be more than fine getting qualified tenants.

Chapter 10

Screening Section 8 Tenants

YOU SHOULD ONLY CONSIDER APPLICANTS WHO HAVE A voucher in hand, as many will falsely claim to possess one. I recommend requesting that they send you a photo of their voucher via email or text message for verification. Additionally, you will need to conduct a screening, which usually costs around $40, though this may vary depending on the platform you use. I require that all potential tenants be pre-approved, meaning they must provide the necessary documentation before any property viewings.

Often, you will encounter applicants who refuse to pay the screening fee without first viewing the property. In such cases, it's best to move on. As mentioned in an earlier chapter, investing in professional photos and a link to a virtual walkthrough of your property should provide potential tenants with enough information to determine if your property is the right fit for them.

The primary goal of this approach is to limit showings and reduce additional fees from your property manager, while also streamlining the process. For my 21 properties, I've typically shown a house to a maximum of two different tenants at a time. Once a Section 8 tenant completes the entire process, they are usually committed to renting, especially if your property is a five-star option. That's why we focus on these types of homes; they attract tenants easily, and tenants are more willing to pay the screening fee for five-star properties. Occasionally, I receive applications from tenants that I do not select because another candidate was a better fit or submitted their application earlier. I keep their information on file for future consideration.

When setting up the screening, you can specify the information you want to collect. For me, I look for a driver's license, pay stub, voucher, credit score, and eviction history. The service performs thorough checks, including searches for sex offender and terrorist registries across all states. You might wonder why I consider credit scores even when applicants have vouchers. I find that a decent credit score often reflects an applicant's responsibility, which is crucial since I'm entrusting them with my property. I strongly advise avoiding tenants with eviction records. Tenants with prior evictions may have a history of not meeting lease agreements, which increases the likelihood of future issues, such as missed rent payments or lease violations. In summary, while every individual situation may vary, avoiding tenants with eviction histories can help you maintain a stable and profitable rental property.

Screening Section 8 Tenants Guide

A guide that helps you ask the questions to get the information you need from prospect Section 8 tenants so you can make the best decision.

https://bit.ly/3Y8qfYf

Chapter 11

Onboarding Section 8 Tenants

YOU'VE COMPLETED THE TENANT SCREENING, and now it's time to onboard them. Let's break down how that process works. The tenant toured the property with your property manager, loved it, and is ready to proceed. Congratulations!

At this stage, you might have your property manager conduct a walkthrough of the tenant's current home. The purpose of this is to assess the condition of their existing living space. Ideally, you're looking for signs of cleanliness and care; if the tenant's home is messy or in poor condition, it could indicate how they may treat your property.

If they maintain their current home poorly, it's likely they'll treat your property the same way. I utilized this approach for my first three tenant inspections, as it was a service offered by my property manager. However, not all property management companies provide this option, so be sure to clarify this during your negotiations with them. I don't do this as often now, but it's definitely something you should consider when you're just starting out.

After the tenant walks through the property, they might point out maintenance issues that need attention—like a missing mirror in the bathroom or a light that's not working in one of the rooms. It's essential to ensure these items are addressed before they move in.

You should communicate with the tenant, "From this point forward, the timeline will be approximately 60 to 90 days." Ideally, for newcomers, it should be between 30 and 60 days, with a maximum of 60 days, but it's wise to give them a broader timeframe to account for any potential delays, such as permit approvals or unforeseen issues. Generally, tenants familiar with the Section 8 process understand it can take several months.

I often say, "You may not hear from me for about a month, but I will check in with you in the next six weeks to update you on our progress." I've mentioned 60 to 90 days before, only to call them two weeks later with everything already completed.

It's crucial to ensure that your tenants are satisfied with their new home. Happy tenants not only add value but also make the property management process smoother. When tenants are content, they're less likely to move out. Conversely, if they move in with unresolved issues, they may leave sooner, which can lead to more complications and additional costs. I've learned this from personal experience.

Chapter 12

How to Work with Contractors and Vendors

NEXT, I'LL COVER HOW TO EFFECTIVELY COLLABORATE with contractors and vendors, which is vital for building a successful and scalable portfolio.

We've just onboarded a Section 8 tenant and submitted their application. The first step in this process is the Section 8 inspection. An inspector from the relevant housing authority will reach out to you within two to four weeks, depending on the housing authority. They'll contact you via email or phone to schedule a suitable time for the inspection.

Establishing your own vendor network is essential. It's crucial to have your own contacts instead of relying on an overburdened property manager who is juggling multiple requests. To find contractors and vendors, I typically start with Thumbtack or a simple internet search. I look for whatever service I need—be it tree removal, pest control, contractors, handymen, or maintenance technicians.

When I worked with a property manager who lacked an in-house maintenance team, every request I submitted resulted in them sending out a third-party vendor. I often found myself calling the property manager, who didn't always answer. Frustrated, I asked for the vendor's contact information so I could communicate directly. Once I started working directly with the vendor, I realized I didn't need to rely on a property manager who wasn't providing good customer service.

This approach helped me build a reliable network of vendors. After moving away from that property management company, I reached out to these vendors and said, "I'm no longer working with [property management company], but you were fantastic on all our requests. I'd like to continue collaborating with you directly. Can I pay you myself?" If you're a good client and easy to work with, they're usually more than happy to accommodate.

Now, I have a list of trusted vendors, including a roofer, couple of plumbers, several general contractors, a pest control specialist, landscaper, etc. I'm continually refining my vendor list, as it's wise to have multiple options. Timing conflicts can arise, and it's crucial to get work done promptly—after all, time is money.

It's essential to understand that in the maintenance, rehab, and construction industries, it is standard practice to pay approximately 50% upfront for a job. For instance, if you're hiring someone for a $10,000 job involving painting and minor remodeling, you would typically provide $5,000 upfront. This helps them cover initial expenses, such as hiring workers and purchasing materials.

As you build a relationship with a contractor and bring them more work, they may start to waive the upfront payments because they know you and are more trusting. However, when you're just starting out and making a name for yourself, upfront payments will probably be necessary.

I also advise using a credit card for payments when working with a brand-new vendor. I'm grateful I did this once when I needed to remove some trees. I found two highly rated contractors on Thumbtack, but unfortunately, both ended up ghosting me after I paid them half of the $4,000 job, which amounted to $2,000. They claimed they were busy and in the hospital. Thankfully, because I had paid with a credit card, I was able to secure a refund.

I typically use Zelle for trusted vendors, as it allows for quick payments and is often their preferred method. However, many vendors may not have a credit card payment portal set up. If you encounter a vendor who does, especially on your first transaction, I strongly recommend using a credit card. This provides an added layer of protection. For instance, if I had paid the vendors who ghosted me via Zelle, I would have lost my money, as Zelle transactions are nonrefundable. Therefore, always opt to pay with a credit card.

When you are prompt, easy to work with, and pay on time, you can get things done efficiently. This is especially important when managing properties remotely, as you need to influence and expedite tasks from afar. Building a trusted vendor network is key, and trust is cultivated by timely payments and straightforward communication. If work falls short of standards, address the issue with the vendor to find a mutually beneficial resolution.

Being stingy or delaying payments won't help you establish a reliable network, especially when you're not on-site every day. You need dependable people who can act quickly. For example, just last night at 10 p.m. (Sunday), I received a request from a tenant moving in on Monday. The house wasn't ready because they wanted a garage door opener installed. I texted my contractor, explained the urgency, and he agreed to rearrange his schedule to get it done. As a result, my tenant will be satisfied upon moving in the next day.

If I were a difficult client who didn't pay promptly, I wouldn't have been able to secure help on such short notice. Vendors are more likely to prioritize your requests when they know you appreciate their work and compensate them fairly. In remote property management, this is essential for success.

I own 21 properties across the country, which can be daunting. I often wonder what I can do from afar if something goes wrong. That's why having a trusted network on the ground is essential. When managing major renovations or construction projects, it's crucial to have someone on-site to oversee the work. I typically have relied on a property manager for this, and while my experiences with property managers have been mixed, my most recent one excelled at providing detailed walkthroughs.

In the past, I trusted a contractor too much, and unfortunately, their work consistently failed inspections. This experience taught me an important lesson: you must have the contractor who remodeled or worked on your properties present at all inspections until their work passes inspections. You should stipulate that a full payment will only be released once all inspections are passed.

Initially, I sent the payment based on a video they provided, which looked good. However, I later discovered multiple issues during the inspections. Eventually, I had to find a new contractor who guarantees their work will pass inspection and ensures they are present for each inspection.

I must admit that when I first started, I opted for the cheapest contractor, which ended up costing me not only money but also valuable time dealing with various issues. Now, I have a trusted contractor and a reliable team on the ground to provide an extra set of eyes and ears, ensuring the work meets my standards.

When starting out, it's essential to set clear payment terms in advance: send 50% upfront, 75% upon completion, and the remaining balance after all inspections have been passed. Make sure to document this agreement via email to avoid any disputes later on.

I've had disagreements with my contractor in the past, and while it didn't go well, I was able to refer to our original discussion. For instance, they claimed I owed him for work he said was completed, but the property was clearly unfinished, and I had third party photos and videos confirming. I was able to send photos and videos from my trusted contacts to back up my case. As a remote investor, it's easy for others to take advantage of you since you can't always verify their work, which is why establishing a vetted and trusted network on the ground is crucial.

Once you build your team, scaling and acquiring more properties to increase your cash flow will become much easier as you optimize these processes. I wish I had a resource that clearly outlined inspections, contractor collaboration, and vendor management when I started my journey. I learned all of this over the past four years.

That's why I wrote this book—many other resources lacked the detailed insights I was looking for. I hope this material helps you gain a clearer understanding. I genuinely want to see you succeed in acquiring your own properties and establishing your own team. I go into greater detail in my course *Section 8 in 8 Minutes.*

Chapter 13

Passing Section 8 and Occupancy Inspections

NOW THAT YOUR TEAM IS IN PLACE, you've secured your market, purchased your property, and everything is ready. The next step is passing Section 8 and occupancy inspections.

First, ensure you have a trusted handyman, contractor, property manager, or maintenance technician scheduled to be on-site for the inspection—and make sure they arrive early. Inspectors are known to show up ahead of time, especially if they have cancelations, so it's best to be prepared.

If you're able to, attend the first inspection in person to get a sense of how things work in your market. To ensure I fully understood the experience for my first property, I flew out specifically to observe the process and recorded it for my YouTube channel (https://youtu.be/Qg91daUtg54?si=HPS4oLsGHbSsWrTD).

It's important to approach the inspection as if you're in a job interview. Be courteous, and personable—maybe even throw in a light joke or two. Arrive early and maintain an easy-going attitude. Building a good rapport with the inspector can make a big difference in how smoothly things go.

Having been in this industry for a few years, I'm now very familiar with the inspection process and know what inspectors look for. When I was just starting out, the process was much slower, and I struggled to schedule and pass inspections, which delayed tenant move-ins. My unfamiliarity with the requirements caused setbacks. But now, I can schedule inspections much faster, typically within one to two weeks.

I believe this is because I've built a rapport with the inspectors—they know me, they know my properties are well-maintained, and they trust I'm serious about my business. There are usually only three to four inspectors per housing authority, so you'll work with the same people repeatedly for initial and annual inspections.

Before your first inspection, make sure all utilities are on and check that both interior and exterior outlets work properly. Inspectors will test every outlet using a circuit analyzer. Additionally, all windows should function and lock securely.

For flooring, you can't have any cracked or lifted tiles, hardwood, or laminate. Inspectors aren't concerned with the aesthetics; they're focused on safety, mainly ensuring there's no tripping hazard.

Plumbing and utilities have to be on because again, you have to run the hot and cold water. During the inspection, they'll check every faucet and sink, including the P-trap, ensuring they're sealed properly with no gaps into the walls. You're required to provide a fridge and stove/oven, but other appliances like dishwashers, garbage disposals, and washers/dryers are optional for Section 8. I recommend that they be removed to avoid extra maintenance costs, especially dishwashers as those tend to breakdown easily.

Other basics include a working smoke detector in each room and a CO2 monitor is required on every property. If you have a multiple story property, you may need to install a CO2 monitor on each floor. I usually install two to be safe.

For the walls, they must be smooth, clean, and free from holes or mold. Once, I tried to pass an inspection with walls that could have used a paint job but weren't terrible. The inspector required a full repaint, which cost $2,400, but I had anticipated that as a potential expense before passing the inspection. You'll most likely need to repaint the interior after each move-out, but if the condition is still good, you might get by with just minor touch-ups in key areas.

For the HVAC and water heater, inspectors will turn on both the furnace and AC to ensure they work, testing temperatures as low as 60°F and as high as 78° F. They'll also check for rust or corrosion on the water heater. In many of my properties, the water heater area often has rust or dirt build-up, so I always have my maintenance team clean and repaint the area to improve its appearance.

It's essential to remove all trash and debris, making sure the house is clean and presentable. For the exterior, the gutters need to be clear, and the roof must be in good condition, with no gaps or openings for water or pests to enter. It should also be free of mold or mildew. I've had properties with green mold on the exterior, which required power washing to pass inspection.

Additionally, when scoping out homes for inspection, make sure there are no tree branches touching the house or hanging over the roof. This can be costly to address, but it's important to tackle it before purchasing or scheduling an inspection.

The housing voucher program requires an annual inspection, and I highly recommend having your property manager or handyman conduct a walkthrough before it takes place. I made the mistake of trusting the tenant when they assured me everything would be cleaned and fixed. However, when the inspector arrived, there were several issues flagged. You don't want to rely on the tenant's view of what acceptable housing looks like. The inspector's assessment is final, so it's best to ensure everything is in order beforehand.

When I talk about aiming for five-star properties, it's because too many people are doing Section 8 on rundown, 1880s homes in the city where everything is old, creaky, and patched together. While these properties may seem like a bargain due to their low price, they often come with numerous issues that make it hard to pass Section 8 inspections. These properties frequently end up in abatement. I recently had a family contact me whose house was in abatement, and they transferred their voucher to me as the new landlord and moved into one of my properties.

Abatement occurs when a property fails too many inspections, forcing the tenant to move out, and the rental payments stop until the house is brought back up to code. I've never had this happen, but it's a risk if your property doesn't pass inspections.

Once you pass the inspection, you're all set—congrats! Typically, right after the inspection, they'll provide you with the HAP (Housing Assistance Payments) contract. This document outlines the approved rent amount, what the housing authority will pay, and the tenant's portion. For example, it might say, "You've been approved for $1,000 a month. The tenant's portion will be $100, and the housing authority will pay $900. Sign the document."

After that, you can contact the tenant to confirm their move-in date.

Turnkey/Section 8 Inspection Checklist

This document contains the main components a Section 8 inspector is going to check and look for. You would send this document to your property manager/handyman or whoever is on site during your inspections.

https://bit.ly/4gNwkBR

Chapter 14

Managing Tenants Moving Forward

Once you've passed the inspection and the tenant is ready to move in, it's time to focus on managing your tenant. The first step is having them sign the lease. While you can find a generic lease online, I wouldn't recommend it—especially if you're using a property manager, which I assume you are, particularly if you're just starting out. Property managers typically use leases tailored to the specific market, which can make a big difference.

For example, in St. Louis, there's an important detail regarding utilities, specifically the sewer. By law, the sewer must be in the landlord's name, but I include a clause in the lease stating that the tenant will be billed for it monthly. If it's not clearly outlined in the lease, the landlord becomes responsible for that utility. These kinds of market-specific details are why I suggest using your property manager's lease and ensuring all utilities are properly assigned to the tenant.

If you're paying your property manager to handle tenant screening, that service is typically included in their fee, usually the equivalent of one month's rent as commission. However, since I handle my own tenant listings, I pay separately for the lease service.

This is just my approach, and your experience may vary depending on your property manager. It's important to understand exactly what services your property manager provides. For example, I used to pay a $250 lease fee because I managed everything else related to tenants' screening and selection, but I preferred using the property manager's lease. This way, if an eviction or other legal issue arises, the property manager is familiar with enforcing their own lease.

It's crucial to ensure the lease outlines that utilities are either separate or billed back to the tenant. If something isn't clear, ask your property manager to specify exactly what's included and what's not. When it's time for the tenant to move in, make sure they understand they can't take possession until all utilities are transferred into their name, as outlined in the lease. I rarely have issues with tenants handling this, though sometimes you might receive a prorated utility bill for the first week or two due to the transfer process. You can simply add that to the tenant's next month's rent.

Regarding the security deposit, it's generally one month's rent, so if the rent is $1,300, the deposit is also $1,300. However, I've adjusted this for some of my Section 8 tenants who may have financial challenges. Now, if their credit score is over 600, I lower the deposit to $1,000. You can stick to the full month's rent for the deposit, or your property manager may suggest an amount based on the local market.

If their credit score is below 600, I increase the security deposit to $1,500, and tenants understand this. You should understand your local regulations. Generally, the typical security deposit is equivalent to one month's rent.

In St. Louis, for example, the housing authority can cap security deposits at $1,500, so even if the rent is $1,800, you can't charge more than $1,500 for the deposit. Again, this varies by market, so it's essential to know how it is in your market, but the typical security deposit is one month of rent.

Currently, I don't allow pets. If you decide to allow them, you can charge a non-refundable pet fee, usually between $300 and $500 per pet. Personally, I don't permit pets because my properties are nicely remodeled, and I'm not ready to deal with the additional wear and tear they can cause. If you choose to allow pets, ask your property manager or you collect a copy of the pet owner's ID and include a clause in the lease specifying the terms of pet ownership.

When the tenant moves in, your property manager typically conducts a move-in inspection to document the property's condition. There should be a move-in checklist or documentation provided by the property manager. If they don't have one, be sure to request it. This documentation is critical when the tenant eventually moves out—it ensures that anything not noted at move-in is their responsibility to repair.

It's important to have direct contact information for your tenants. One of the biggest challenges I've faced is poor communication between tenants and property managers. In several cases, tenants would submit a request, and the property manager would take weeks to respond. Imagine dealing with something like a broken faucet for three weeks without any action. This lack of responsiveness prompted me to take on more property management tasks myself.

I now make it clear to tenants that if they don't receive support in a timely manner, they should contact me directly. It's crucial to ensure that they feel heard and supported.

Before my tenants move in, I give them my contact information. I tell them, "If you're having any issues and the property manager isn't responding or things are getting out of hand, please escalate the issue to me directly." This has really helped resolve a lot of potential problems. Good communication with tenants is key because you'll need to coordinate various tasks such as inspections, pre-inspections, appraisals, and more.

For example, when refinancing properties, you'll need to arrange for insurance companies and bank appraisers to access the home, and responsive tenants make this process much smoother. Having great communication with tenants is essential for keeping things running smoothly.

When starting out, you may rely heavily on property managers, but it's crucial to build your own vendor network. Property management teams don't always have the best vendors, and this can lead to delays in resolving tenant issues. A happy tenant is more likely to stay longer, which helps keep turnover costs low in the long run. Additionally, using your own vendors is cheaper than relying solely on the property manager's team, saving you money.

I recommend setting a $500 limit for maintenance requests with your property manager. This means that if a repair or maintenance issue arises and the cost is estimated to exceed $500, your property manager must get your approval before moving forward. For example, if a work order comes in and the repair is estimated to be over $500, they are required to contact me first to see if I want to proceed or use my vendor. For anything under $500, I typically allow them to handle it without needing my approval.

The reason for the $500 limit is that my cash flow averages around $500 to $600 per property. By setting this limit, I ensure that I'm still earning some cash flow even when there are maintenance costs. If you're only cash flowing $200 to $300 per property, it doesn't leave much room for handling maintenance expenses, so having a healthy cash flow buffer is important.

This limit also allows you to monitor the types of maintenance issues coming up in your properties, which helps you decide whether to use your own vendors or continue relying on the property manager's team. Some landlords prefer to review every request, while others may choose to let the property manager handle everything for the sake of convenience.

Ultimately, investing in a quality, well- maintained property can save you money and time in the long run.

A five-star property reduces the likelihood of frequent maintenance issues, helps maintain tenant satisfaction, and ensures your investment runs smoothly.

Chapter 15

Mistakes I Made That You Can Learn From

I MUST ADMIT, IT'S HUMBLING to share these experiences because some of them are embarrassing. But I've always wanted to be a transparent guide who's not afraid to discuss mistakes openly. My goal with this chapter is that you learn through my mistakes. A lot of so-called *gurus* paint themselves as perfect, without showing you the messy behind-the-scenes stuff. If you're just starting out with $25,000, you want to make sure you're fully aware of the risks, the potential pitfalls, and the right decisions to make—especially when this may be all the capital you have—I wish I had this kind of insight when I first started.

One mistake I made early on was buying multiple homes at once, all with below-market rents. These tenants were paying below market rates, and I knew I could make significantly more if I placed Section 8 tenants. However, I was eager to grow my portfolio and ended up purchasing these eight properties at around $16,000 down payment for each, for $130,000. I finally had some money to invest and went a little overboard, buying all eight homes at once.

At the time, I thought the numbers made sense— each mortgage was $450, and the rent was $850. I knew the properties could eventually rent for $1,400 to $1,500 under Section 8, so I figured I'd eventually increase my income.

In the meantime, I was making about $400 a month per home, and after management fees, around $300 per property. With eight homes, that came to about $2,400 a month. But this taught me the importance of having a better cash flow forecast and more cushion for unexpected expenses. It's crucial to aim for the highest rent-to-mortgage spread possible to give yourself breathing room.

First off, if you've ever dealt with market tenants in lower-income areas, you know that timely rent payments can be unpredictable. This is why I prefer Section 8, not just for the higher rent, but because the payments are guaranteed. With Section 8, the rent is deposited directly into your account on the first of each month, whereas with market tenants, you can never be certain if or when the rent will come through. The reliability of Section 8 rent ensures steady cash flow, which is critical.

Out of the eight properties I bought, only one tenant consistently paid rent on time. This led to a series of evictions after trying to negotiate payment plans. Some tenants were two or three months behind. While purchasing these homes, I had access to the ledgers and information, but the data wasn't as transparent as I thought—it was somewhat *fudged*. As a result, on four of the properties, I didn't receive any rent for several months while transitioning management, waiting on payments, and ultimately evicting tenants.

On top of that, since I failed to inspect the properties properly, I ended up spending $10,000 to $15,000 per house to get them rent-ready.

I also underestimated the time it would take to complete the turnovers since I didn't have the team in place that I have now. Eventually, I got everything sorted out, and five of the eight properties are now rented through Section 8, earning me over $1,500 each. Now, I'm cash flowing more than I was when they were rented at $850.

From this experience, I've learned that it's crucial to buy vacant properties that can command top market rents while maximizing cash flow, as unexpected issues and costs are inevitable. I used to wonder why owners sold instead of simply raising rents; it's challenging to increase rents, attract quality tenants, and pass inspections—especially from a distance.

While I've gained valuable insights from this journey, I regret my initial eagerness to grow my portfolio, which led me to take unnecessary risks. My advice for beginners is to avoid purchasing properties with market tenants, below-market rents, or located in low-income areas unless they are Section 8. A seemingly good deal on paper may not be worth the hassle.

I would suggest starting with vacant properties only, certainly one at a time. I wish I had just gone one at a time and followed this process that I've created now. I estimated around $110,000 I spent in lost money, lost rents, the money I spent turning over the units.

I haven't even calculated the time I spent on the weekends just finding vendors and things like that. Do not buy multiple homes all at once with under market rents before you have the team in place. Now, if I took on a project like this today, it would look a lot different.

Fortunately, I could refinance every property in that portfolio, and I could take back whatever down payment I spent, which was about $16,000 each. I got $16,000 or more back per property. Some were $19,000, some were $21,000, some were $20,000. Luckily, the money I spent on them, I got back through a cash out refi, but this portfolio would have been a terrible loss had I not been able to refinance all eight properties.

Next, I learned a painful lesson when I ignored significant basement issues during an inspection. As a new investor, I was excited to buy a three-bedroom property for just $55,000, thinking it was a great deal. However, I overlooked the basement's poor condition, not realizing its importance as part of the foundation, especially in the Midwest, where basements are critical.

There was water infiltration, and without a reliable team to assess the costs and solutions, I ended up spending around $12,000 on repairs before finally finding a waterproofing specialist who charged an additional $10,000. Ignoring these basement issues ultimately cost me $22,000 and over a year of time. I was caught up in my excitement about purchasing properties, envisioning cash flow from a mortgage of only $420 against potential rents of $1,300 to $1,400.

This experience underscores the importance of thoroughly inspecting properties and hiring professionals when necessary. Always invest in proper inspections from the start to avoid costly mistakes.

A year later, I see that my three-bedroom properties are renting for $1,500 to $1,600, so I initially envisioned this property as a potential cash cow, possibly generating an extra $1,000 a month in cash flow. However, I overlooked the significant basement issues that ultimately disqualified it as a true turnkey investment. This property then also became my worst rental amount, bringing in only $950 a month—a disappointing reality that highlighted the importance of having a healthy cash flow spread.

In hindsight, had I used seller financing with an $800/month mortgage while only receiving $950 in rent, it would have been a financial strain. This experience taught me that low rents can happen, so it's crucial to purchase properties with solid financial fundamentals. The area of Jennings, despite initially passing my criteria, isn't one I'd choose again and was my only property in my portfolio that did not receive at least 80% of the HUD FMR estimated Section 8 rent.

As a comparison, I have a two-bedroom property generating $1,025 a month in rent, while the three bedroom is stuck at $950. This is a significant lesson: if something feels off or *fishy*, it's better to walk away and find another opportunity. The basement, which looked like a makeshift lab with red paint and cords everywhere, was a major red flag. I learned not to ignore basement conditions, especially as a California native unfamiliar with their importance in the Midwest.

Another mistake I made was not holding my contractor accountable by having a second independent person review the work. My general contractor would claim to have done the work and send me photos and videos, which I accepted without thorough inspection because the photos looked good. I would then pay him in full before the properties passed inspection, relying solely on what I saw in those images. Unsurprisingly, the properties didn't pass inspection.

When I asked him to be present during inspections, he struggled to understand the inspection reports. These documents outline the issues that need to be addressed to pass, but he couldn't interpret them. This experience taught me the importance of having someone who can accurately read inspection reports and knows how to address the identified issues.

Additionally, some unexpected problems arose I couldn't have predicted. This is why it's crucial to ensure a healthy cash flow, as unforeseen expenses will inevitably occur. For instance, one of my properties had a large tree, and a branch fell, damaging a neighbor's garage. Unfortunately, this too cut into my budget.

One unforeseen issue arose with one of my best properties when a tenant encountered a neighbor with a vicious dog—possibly a pit bull—that was always roaming into my yard. The dog was on a long leash, allowing it access to both neighboring yards despite my three-foot chain-link fence. Previous workers had warned me about the dog, but rather than confront the neighbor, I chose to eliminate the risk and liability.

I installed an $8,500 privacy fence to ensure the tenant felt safe before moving in. Given that this property generates over $1,100 a month in cash flow, I knew I would recoup the cost in about eight months. More importantly, this investment not only protected me from potential lawsuits but also enhanced tenant satisfaction by providing privacy. I've learned that I can't rely on neighbors to treat my tenants well; I must proactively safeguard my business. The expense was significant, but with healthy cash flow and 5-star properties, I was able to manage it.

With 21 properties under my belt, I can honestly say I've made my share of mistakes. My hope with this book is to give you insight so that you don't make the same mistakes I made and are one step closer to your financial dream. It's been quite a journey!

Chapter 16

Taxes and LLC Information

FOR LEGAL CLARITY, LET ME EMPHASIZE I am not a licensed tax advisor or legal professional. It's important to consult with a qualified professional regarding your specific situation. The information I provide is intended for entertainment purposes only; please seek advice from your financial advisors, attorneys, or insurance representatives.

Now that we have that out of the way, let's dive into some general tax and LLC information. Since this topic is highly circumstantial, I'll keep it high-level.

Foremost, it's crucial to avoid holding rental properties in your personal name. The U.S. is known for its litigious environment, meaning that if something goes wrong—such as a lack of safety features—you could be personally liable. If the property is held in your name, plaintiffs can sue you directly, putting your personal assets at risk. Conversely, if your rental property is held in an LLC, any legal actions would be limited to the LLC and its assets, protecting your personal holdings.

A common practice is to establish an LLC, open a bank account under that LLC, and manage all payments and leases through the business. This approach helps to further shield your personal assets from potential liabilities associated with your rental properties.

While the topic can be quite intricate, the key takeaway is that you should place any rental properties in an LLC to limit liability. When setting up your LLC, ensure you open a separate bank account for all transactions related to the property. When filling out the Section 8 application, be sure to list yourself as the manager of the LLC, even if you are also the owner. This establishes you as the controlling party while keeping your personal interests separate.

Initially, I made the mistake of using my personal accounts for transactions, but now I've established distinct accounts, credit cards, and credit lines in the LLC's name. It's essential to consistently represent yourself as the manager of the LLC to avoid *piercing the corporate veil.*

Many people overlook the importance of clearly separating business and personal expenses. If you intermingle these accounts—such as using LLC funds for personal expenses—there's a risk that, in the event of a lawsuit, the court may determine you've pierced the corporate veil. This means they could pursue you personally, despite the LLC structure.

Always maintain a professional approach and manage all transactions through the LLC to safeguard your personal assets. When I first started, I wasn't fully aware of these nuances and mistakenly used my personal name, but now I understand the importance of keeping everything separate to protect myself legally.

The goal is to operate your real estate ventures like a legitimate business. This is crucial because, if any issues arise, and your records reveal questionable transactions—like using LLC funds for personal purchases, such as Nike shoes or food deliveries—it can jeopardize your liability protection. This practice is known as *piercing the corporate veil*, and you want to avoid it at all costs.

As I mentioned in an earlier chapter, holding properties in an LLC can present challenges, particularly when financing properties under $100,000. This is why it's important to seek investor-friendly lenders. When discussing financing options, ask if you can deed the property from your personal name to the LLC or if you can close in the LLC's name. Personally, I prefer to buy properties in my name to keep costs down. After purchasing, I then transfer the property to my LLC for about $400 in legal fees.

While the mortgage liability remains with me, meaning that a default could personally affect my credit, legal protection is in place for any lawsuits, as the properties are managed under the LLC's name. Tenants sign leases with my LLC (like St. Louis LLC1, St. Louis LLC2), making it clear that the LLC is the landlord of record. This structure helps insulate my personal assets from potential liabilities associated with the rental properties.

I always identify myself as the manager or one of the property managers, which is why I emphasized finding investor-friendly lenders. If you can purchase and close in an LLC, that's ideal. A lawyer advised me to set up a separate LLC and bank account for each property, but since these properties are valued between $60,000 and $70,000, I grouped four properties into one LLC. This approach simplifies management and reduces maintenance costs for the LLCs, as managing 21 separate LLCs would be cumbersome and costly. Additionally, tax professionals often charge around $1,000+ per LLC for tax preparation, which adds up.

It's essential to consult licensed professionals because many first-time investors, especially W- 2 employees, may not fully grasp investment and tax strategies. Since I've been in this for a few years, I recommend holding properties for at least one to two years before diving into more complex strategies like refinancing to understand their impact better.

It's essential to consult with a licensed tax professional when navigating complex financial matters. The topics can become intricate, involving holding companies, offshore accounts, trusts, and irrevocable trusts, all tailored to your specific circumstances. I've shared some high-level insights and tax strategies I've found useful, but a professional can provide the personalized guidance necessary for your situation.

Chapter 17

Conclusion

IN CONCLUSION, PURSUING YOUR GOALS IN LIFE requires taking risks and making informed decisions. You may be more prepared than you realize. Throughout my journey, I encountered many property managers and realtors who said I was approaching things incorrectly, but I'm grateful I challenged their assumptions.

I remember my first property manager telling me I could rent my home for $900 a month. However, I thought Section 8 could yield $1,200. They insisted that wasn't possible, claiming they managed 500 properties and found Section 8 unreliable. I decided to take a chance, and instead of a $900 tenant, I rented it for $1,185 on Section 8. That success prompted that same property manager to accept Section 8 tenants in all their properties. This experience taught me I had a better understanding of Section 8 than many in the industry.

Your first property is crucial. While it may not transform your life overnight, it marks the beginning of your investment journey. I now own 21 properties, a journey that started five years ago with two years of research and networking before I purchased my first property. Now, I'm sharing what I've learned along the way.

You need to be fully committed to this journey. Ask yourself: how badly do you want this? If you're only half-hearted about it, I recommend holding off on starting. Real estate requires dedication.

I approached my real estate journey like this: I was prepared to invest four years without guaranteed income, much like attending college. In college, you gain knowledge, expecting it will pay off later. I adopted a similar mindset for real estate; if it didn't pan out in four years, I could always sell my portfolio.

It's unrealistic to think you'll instantly replace your income when you start. That didn't happen in your day job, nor did it happen during college. In my first year, I was hopeful about making some money, but now, three years later, I've retired my partner, and we live by the beach. Real estate can provide for you, but your success hinges on your commitment.

When starting out, don't expect to earn the most money immediately. Initially, my cash flow from properties was only $300 to $400, but now it consistently ranges from $700 to $800.

I recently achieved an $1,100 cash flow on one of my properties, a milestone I couldn't have reached without first starting with a property that only cash flowed $300.

Initially, I didn't have a comprehensive course to guide me through this process. While I purchased some general information, it lacked the detailed, day-to-day insights I needed. This gap inspired me to write this book and create a course. If I had access to this kind of information earlier, I would have saved a significant amount of time and potentially hundreds of thousands of dollars.

With my course, Section 8 in 8 Minutes, you'll learn to underwrite a property in eight minutes or less, allowing you to quickly decide whether to move forward. My goal is to educate and empower you to make swift, informed decisions that can shape your financial future.

About the Author

Andre Calloway Cazares stands at the forefront of the global technology sales arena, a titan in Section 8 real estate investment, and a voice that shapes the industry through his published works. His story is one of remarkable ascent from the humble beginnings of a cell phone sales rep from East Los Angeles to a revered Global Technology Sales Representative whose career has spanned the nation. Now, he brings his wealth of experience back to Los Angeles, where he lives with his family, grounded in the community that shaped him.

Raised amidst the challenges of a family dependent on government assistance, Andre's early life was deeply influenced by the realities of WIC, food stamps, and Section 8 housing. These experiences did not define him; instead, they sparked a fierce determination to redefine the narrative around Section 8 housing—turning it into a beacon of opportunity for investors and a source of quality living for tenants. He aims to elevate Section 8 real estate investing from a niche market to a cornerstone of financial freedom and societal contribution.

Section 8 Free Housing Calculator

Use my *Section 8 Rental Property Calculator* to identify how many rental properties you require to pay for your monthly housing expense. This allows you to live for free.

https://bit.ly/3YdzTtI